Reforming the Bank
Regulatory Structure

Reforming the Bank Regulatory Structure

A Staff Paper by Andrew S. Carron

THE BROOKINGS INSTITUTION
Washington, D.C.

© 1984 by
THE BROOKINGS INSTITUTION
1775 Massachusetts Avenue., N.W., Washington, D.C. 20036

Library of Congress Catalogue Card Number 84-72355
ISBN 0-8157-1303-7

1 2 3 4 5 6 7 8 9

THE BROOKINGS INSTITUTION is an independent organization devoted to nonpartisan research, education, and publication in economics, government, foreign policy, and the social sciences generally. Its principal purposes are to aid in the development of sound public policies and to promote public understanding of issues of national importance.

The Institution was founded on December 8, 1927, to merge the activities of the Institute for Government Research, founded in 1916, the Institute of Economics, founded in 1922, and the Robert Brookings Graduate School of Economics and Government, founded in 1924.

The Board of Trustees is responsible for the general administration of the Institution, while the immediate direction of the policies, program, and staff is vested in the President, assisted by an advisory committee of the officers and staff. The by-laws of the Institution state: "It is the function of the Trustees to make possible the conduct of scientific research, and publication, under the most favorable conditions, and to safeguard the independence of the research staff in the pursuit of their studies and in the publication of the results of such studies. It is not a part of their function to determine, control, or influence the conduct of particular investigations or the conclusions reached."

The President bears final responsibility for the decision to publish a manuscript as a Brookings book. In reaching his judgment on the competence, accuracy, and objectivity of each study, the President is advised by the director of the appropriate research program and weighs the views of a panel of expert outside readers who report to him in confidence on the quality of the work. Publication of a work signifies that it is deemed a competent treatment worthy of public consideration but does not imply endorsement of conclusions or recommendations.

The Institution maintains its position of neutrality on issues of public policy in order to safeguard the intellectual freedom of the staff. Hence interpretations or conclusions in Brookings publications should be understood to be solely those of the authors and should not be attributed to the Institution, to its trustees, officers, or other staff members, or to the organizations that support its research.

Foreword

THE DEVELOPMENT of financial institutions in the United States has been accompanied by a parallel expansion of government regulation. As banks and other intermediaries evolved into more varied and sophisticated forms, federal laws established new agencies specialized by industry and function. The regulatory system has grown from one federal bank regulator a century ago to ten federal agencies with some jurisdiction over financial services. Since the earliest years of regulation, firms in the same industry have been regulated by different agencies, and any given firm has been subject to the overlapping control of several regulators.

Proposals to consolidate and rationalize the federal regulation of financial services have been forthcoming in a nearly continuous stream ever since there were agencies to consolidate. Yet the system has become even more complex. Regulations have overlapped and have left gaps. Agencies have quarreled over regulatory policy. The problems have become especially acute in recent years with the lessening of traditional distinctions among industries.

An alternative view maintains that a concentration of regulatory power would promote conservatism, retard innovation, and discriminate against certain classes of institutions. Indeed, even critics of the current structure have not found evidence of major costs imposed on society, at least in the past.

The debate over regulatory reform assumed new currency in 1984. First came the recommendations of the Task Group on Regulation of Financial Services under Vice President Bush. Composed of the heads of the major financial regulatory agencies and high executive branch officials, the task group considered the consolidation of bank regulation, the merging of the federal deposit insurance agencies, and the elimination of separate regulation of banks and thrift institutions. Later in the year, difficulties at a major bank and at the country's largest savings and loan association raised serious questions about the agencies' approach to regulation and depositor protection.

This staff paper provides a guide to the reorganization of financial regulation. It is part of a larger Brookings study, "U.S. Financial Markets and Institutions," supported by a grant from the Andrew W. Mellon Foundation. The author conducted part of the research for this paper in preparation of his report for the Federal Home Loan Bank Board under contract 683024.

Andrew S. Carron was a senior fellow in the Brookings Economic Studies program at the time he wrote this paper. He thanks Richard C. Aspinwall, R. Dan Brumbaugh, Samuel B. Chase, Paul M. Horvitz, and John S. Strong for helpful comments on the manuscript. Research assistance was provided by Joy O. Robinson and Shannon P. Butler. Gregg Forte edited the paper, and Carolyn A. Rutsch verified its factual content.

The views expressed here are those of the author and should not be ascribed to the persons or organizations whose assistance is acknowledged or to the trustees, officers or other staff members of the Brookings Institution.

BRUCE K. MACLAURY
President

February 1985
Washington, D.C.

INNOVATION and economic adversity have drastically changed the character of U.S. financial markets in the last half-dozen years. New types of institutions have appeared as long-established types have faded from the scene; traditional distinctions have blurred, and old labels have become inadequate to describe the new activities. In contrast to the industry, the U.S. financial regulatory system has remained static. The aggressive, automated, diversified multibillion-dollar companies that compete in today's financial services industry are regulated by agencies designed for the Civil War, the Panic of 1907, and the Great Depression. Regulatory techniques are outmoded and inconsistent. The system is characterized by overlapping authorities, duplicate controls, conflicts, and omissions. It is a disorderly structure, hard-pressed to cope with continuing changes in the industry.

Today's fragmented structure of financial regulation reflects its piecemeal development over a period of decades. Each new type of market institution brought its own set of regulators. The first commercial bank in the United States received its charter from the Continental Congress in 1781. State chartering also became common and was the only avenue to a bank license during the middle third of the 1800s. A federal role was introduced in the 1860s through the chartering of banks by the Office of the Comptroller of the Currency. The Federal Reserve Act set up a further layer of control in 1913. The Great Depression brought forth government policies to assure stability, protect depositors, and nurture socially desirable investments such as housing. These policies required more controls: federal agencies to regulate stockbrokers and exchanges, insure deposits at commercial and savings banks, and charter and insure deposits at savings and loan associations and credit unions. The Congress extended regulation to mutual funds in 1940, bank holding companies in 1956, all consumer-lending institutions in the 1960s and 1970s, and commodity trading in 1974.

This pattern of development embodies diversity of control and fosters decentralization of economic power. Only recently have the costs of this structure begun to outweigh the benefits. The duplication of authority is now an impediment to effective regulation. The activities of one firm, such as a state chartered, federally insured depository institution, are

1

regulated by a state and a federal agency. Also, two firms that compete with each other, such as a national and a state bank, are each regulated by a different federal agency—the Comptroller of the Currency for the national bank and the Federal Reserve for the state bank.

The specialized structure of regulation led to further specialization of institutions. Lawmakers gave separate roles and regulators to the banking, thrift, securities, and insurance industries, and competition was expected to take place within these industries, not between them. With few exceptions, the regulator for one industry had no authority over firms in another. Federally chartered savings associations have one deposit insurer; banks have a different one; and securities firms another kind of protection altogether. This plan was adequate as long as each firm was content with its assigned niche. For many years, the regulators could keep pace with the few aggressive entrepreneurs who sometimes attempted to break out of this rigid structure.

When the economy and interest rates began their wild gyrations in the 1970s, however, many firms found that new strategies and tactics of competition had become crucial to their survival. Innovation was also spurred by technological advances such as improvements in computers and communications, by regulation-induced distortions in the market, and by new legislation. As this wave of change swept through the financial services industry, large cracks appeared in the federal regulatory structure, and calls for its modernization, although not new, were revived and became more widespread. Many problems were not handled adequately, and the current structure of overlapping, parallel, and specialized agencies was partly to blame. Duplication of control implies higher administrative costs and a greater regulatory burden on firms. Shared responsibility among agencies with differing objectives has led to conflict. Broadened asset and liability powers have engendered new competition between the banking and thrift industries, highlighting differences in regulation and supervision. And the competitive pressures coming from the securities and insurance industries and other financial institutions have spurred the effort to alleviate regulatory rigidities that hamper the responses of thrifts and banks.

Broadly speaking there have been four types of proposals for structural change: First, streamline the parallel state and federal channels for bank and thrift regulation, which are increasingly difficult to coordinate, to cope with a swiftly changing environment and proliferating multistate financial networks; for instance, the importance of federal deposit insurance and Federal Reserve liquidity support should be reflected in the primacy of federal regulators over their state counterparts. Second,

2

reduce the number of federal bank regulatory agencies. Third, consolidate the banking and thrift regulatory structures, a reform intended to accommodate interindustry competition. And fourth, as banks and others expand the range of their services, reduce industry-specific regulation in favor of regulation by function: for example, have one agency handle all deposit insurance and another all securities activity, regardless of the type of firm conducting the activity. The proposal for regulation by function has become especially prominent as unregulated competitors offer services functionally comparable to those of the regulated intermediaries.

The common framework for all of these proposals is the overriding need to maintain the stability of the financial system during and after a reorganization of the regulatory system. Financial market stability, after all, is the fundamental rationale for regulation of banks, thrifts, and securities firms. Financial intermediaries borrow heavily and are more dependent on short-term funds than firms in other sectors; the stable flow of funds needed to support this debt depends on public confidence, which is hard to regain once lost. Problems at one bank or nonbank intermediary can cause difficulties for the rest of the industry if depositors and investors believe—even incorrectly—that other firms are similarly affected. The failure of a bank or other intermediary potentially poses greater harm to the economy than the problems of a similar-size firm in another industry, because contagion can spread rapidly, affecting the money supply, the payment system, government debt, and the federal budget. Hence the emphasis on minimizing risk and promoting public confidence in the regulated intermediaries is important, especially in a transition period.

At the same time, intermediaries are privately owned companies operating for profit. As such, there is a presumption that they should be allowed to experience the results, successful or otherwise, of their decisions. Restrictions on risk taking, such as maintaining high levels of capital, reduce the expected profits of the firm. This creates a dilemma for the regulator, namely, how to promote innovation, growth, and risk taking by individual companies while maintaining stability in the system as a whole. On occasion, excesses of regulatory authority have stifled competition and innovation. In other instances, conflicts, gaps, and overlaps in the regulatory structure have allowed imprudent actions by firms to go unchecked. A measure of regulatory performance, therefore, is the ability to find the proper balance between safety and efficiency-enhancing competition. The structure and organization of the regulatory system can support or hinder the achievement of this balance.

The question of how to organize regulatory agencies should not be considered before, or separately from, the substantive questions of regulation. The preeminent concerns at this time are the asset, liability, and service powers of banks and thrifts; changes in capital requirements; and reform of the deposit insurance system. Agency structure, while important, must be considered in conjunction with these other topics. For example, the question whether banks and thrifts should have the same regulator may be seen to hinge on whether banks and thrifts are going to be accorded similar investment powers. In this analysis the focus remains on agency structure, but the effects of structure on substantive regulation are noted.

After a brief outline of the current financial regulatory structure, this paper analyzes the arguments for and against reorganization and offers recommendations for reform. The focus is primarily on depository institutions—banks and thrifts—and on competition between these firms and the nondepository financial sector.

The Current Financial Regulatory Structure

Government oversight of the financial industry involves licensing (granting charters to qualified firms applying for them), regulation (interpreting the law by issuing rules of operation), supervision (monitoring compliance with regulations through formal examinations), and enforcement (compelling compliance with regulations); hereafter, I will refer to these oversight functions, taken as a whole, as regulation. Government also provides financial support to the industry through deposit insurance and access to emergency funds for companies facing illiquidity.

The following paragraphs are a brief outline (illustrated in figure 1) of the way oversight and financial support are currently organized by the federal and state governments. More detail on the history and operation of these functions is to be found in appendix A.

Office of the Comptroller of the Currency

Congress established the Office of the Comptroller of the Currency in the Treasury Department in 1863 to issue charters to qualified banks that did not wish to come under state regulation. Banks chartered by the Comptroller of the Currency, called national banks, are subject to the agency's regulatory powers.

The Federal Reserve System

The Federal Reserve System was created in 1913 as an independent government agency to stabilize key banking processes and to regulate banks. In its stabilization role it provides nationwide check clearing, lends money to banks belonging to the system, prescribes the level of reserves required of all depository institutions—reserves which became centralized in the system upon its creation—and sets monetary policy, which it executes through the sale and purchase of government securities (open market operations). In its oversight role, the Federal Reserve System has the right to regulate national banks, which are required to join it, but in practice the Comptroller of the Currency remains the primary regulator of national banks. The Federal Reserve is the primary regulator of state chartered member banks[1] and also of bank holding companies regardless of the type of bank the company holds. The Federal Reserve also administers certain consumer protection laws for all depository institutions and, under the terms of the 1933 Glass-Steagall Act, ensures that commercial member banks avoid trading or underwriting corporate securities except as trustees or agents.

The Federal Deposit Insurance Corporation

Banks belonging to the Federal Reserve System automatically receive insurance coverage for their depositors from the Federal Deposit Insurance Corporation, established by Congress in 1933 as an independent government agency. The FDIC has the right to terminate the coverage of any Federal Reserve member bank that it perceives to be excessively risky, after which the bank loses its Federal Reserve membership. FDIC coverage for all other depository institutions is voluntary; it must be approved by the agency and, in the case of state regulated banks, by the state. Although the FDIC has the right to regulate all banks it agrees to insure, in practice it is the primary federal regulator only of state nonmember commercial banks and state savings banks.

The Federal Home Loan Bank Board

Savings and loan associations and savings banks got a new source of credit during the Great Depression when Congress in 1932 created the Federal Home Loan Bank System. To become eligible for the credit,

1. I follow custom in restricting the meaning of the terms *member bank* and *nonmember bank* to describe an institution's Federal Reserve System status.

5

Figure 1. *The Regulation of Banks and Their Holding Companies*

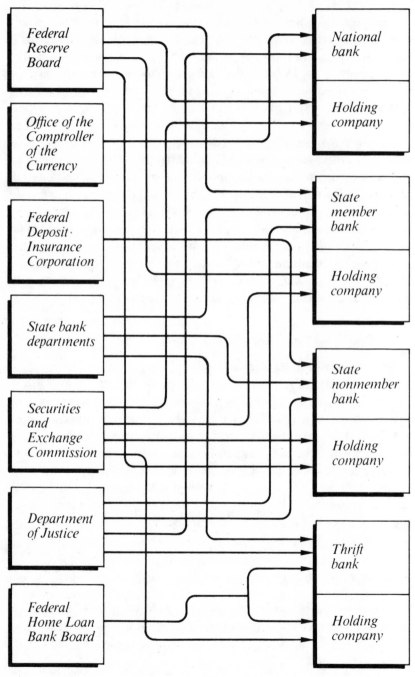

institutions apply to the Federal Home Loan Bank Board for a federal charter, which if granted puts them under FHLBB regulation. The Federal Savings and Loan Insurance Corporation, established in 1934 as part of the FHLBB, insures depositors at all federally chartered savings and loans; state chartered thrifts and mutual savings banks are eligible for coverage.

The National Credit Union Administration

Federal charters for credit unions were created in 1934, after which time several different agencies in succession were designated to charter and regulate those credit unions seeking federal status. The latest of these agencies is the National Credit Union Administration, set up by Congress in 1970. Federally chartered credit unions must take deposit insurance through the NCUA-controlled National Credit Union Share Insurance Fund; state chartered credit unions may choose federal or state deposit insurance coverage or none at all. All credit unions, regardless of charter, have access to emergency credit through another NCUA-controlled unit, the Central Liquidity Facility.

State Bank Departments

State bank departments are the primary regulators of state chartered banks and thrifts that do not belong to the Federal Reserve System. In all other cases, state agencies are secondary to the federal regulator—the Comptroller of the Currency for national banks, the FHLBB for federally chartered savings institutions, the Federal Reserve for state chartered member banks, and the FDIC for state chartered nonmember banks it insures.

Regulatory Powers of Other Agencies

Although financial services firms have many unique characteristics, they also are subject to government regulations that apply to all corporations. However, in matters that fall under both financial and general corporate regulation, the financial regulator often has primary authority.

Depository institutions must obtain approval from their financial regulator for mergers and acquisitions, and the considerations that must be weighed differ from agency to agency. Under the antitrust laws, however, the Justice Department may also review proposed changes in industry structure and may sue to block them.

7

Table 1. *Administrators of Major Consumer Protection Laws as They Apply to Financial Institutions*[a]

Law	Administrator
Community Reinvestment Act of 1977	Primary regulator
Electronic Fund Transfer Act of 1978	Federal Reserve
Equal Credit Opportunity Act	Federal Reserve
Fair Credit Billing Act	Federal Reserve
Fair Credit Reporting Act	Federal Trade Commission
Fair Debt Collections Practices Act	Federal Trade Commission
Fair Housing Act of 1968	Primary regulator
Flood Disaster Protection Act of 1973	Primary regulator
Home Mortgage Disclosure Act of 1975	Federal Reserve
Real Estate Settlement Procedures Act of 1972	Department of Housing and Urban Development
Truth in Lending Act	Federal Reserve

a. Administrators write rules based on the legislation. For each of the consumer protection laws, the enforcement of the rules as they apply to a financial institution is the job of the institution's primary regulator. The primary regulator for national banks is the Office of the Comptroller of the Currency; for state chartered member banks, the Federal Reserve; for state chartered nonmember banks and savings banks, the Federal Deposit Insurance Corporation; for most other thrifts, the Federal Home Loan Bank Board; and for credit unions, the National Credit Union Administration.

Depository institutions are also subject to consumer protection laws. Enforcement of these laws with regard to a financial institution is the function of the institution's primary regulator; but the administration of the laws is in some cases the job of the primary regulator, in others the job of a single agency, as shown in table 1.

Securities, Futures, and Antitrust Regulation

The Securities and Exchange Commission, which dates from 1933, regulates the traders and markets for stocks, bonds, mutual funds, and other financial instruments except commodity futures and certain other types of futures and options. The SEC sets rules for public disclosure by publicly held firms, including bank holding companies, and administers rules for shareholder participation in such firms. The primary regulators of banks and thrifts enforce the functional equivalent of these rules. The SEC also supervises the Securities Investor Protection Corporation, which insures investors against loss or theft of securities housed by brokers.

The Commodity Futures Trading Commission, established in 1974 to handle the rapidly growing futures market, has authority parallel to that of the SEC: it approves futures contracts and options for trading and regulates the market. It also regulates certain stock and bond futures, options on futures contracts, and options on foreign currencies traded on commodity exchanges.

The Issues

The current financial regulatory structure developed in an evolutionary fashion. As existing financial institutions changed, the powers of existing regulatory bodies changed; as new institutions came into being, new agencies were established to deal with them. The resulting pattern is characterized by multiple regulators for depository institutions and consolidated regulation for securities firms. Each decision to adjust the organization of the agencies had its reason, but the resulting composite defies rationality.

However, despite the disorganized structure of financial regulation, it remains to be demonstrated that the structure creates insurmountable problems. After all, there has been no repeat of the Great Depression, and the financial sector has grown rapidly and reasonably efficiently. The following questions will help focus the issue of whether to restructure financial regulation:

—Is the existing structure inherently prone to failure? Does the stability observed to date merely reflect the luck and skill of regulators or the absence of a serious test?

—Is the financial services industry undergoing changes that themselves require rationalization of the regulatory structure?

—What changes in regulatory structure would be necessary and appropriate?

Each possible course of action toward the current structure, including its maintenance, has advantages and disadvantages; in dispute are the magnitudes of the associated benefits and costs. The strong opinions are held by those with direct interests in the outcome—the agencies and the regulated firms—but most of the debates have been couched in terms of public interest. Reform has thus been frustrated both by a failure to agree on the basic merits of the case and by an unwillingness to give up established lines of authority.

The Case for Consolidation

For most of the past fifty years, the financial system has been characterized by rigid separation of its constituent industries; the banking, thrift, and securities sectors were distinct, and regulation of each could proceed independently of the other. Beginning in the mid-1960s, however, and to an increasing extent in recent years, interrelationships have been established.

As seen above in figure 1, there is a complex assignment of responsibilities in the current federal regulatory scheme. One institution may be subject to as many as five regulators, and one regulator may oversee nearly as many different types of institutions. Yet even this diagram understates the degree of complexity; it omits credit unions, securities and commodities dealers, consumer protection controls administered by the Federal Reserve and the Department of Housing and Urban Development, and the subsidiary responsibilities of the Federal Reserve for national banks and of the Federal Deposit Insurance Corporation for national and state member banks. But the case for change in the financial regulatory structure must rest on something more substantial than a desire for a tidy organization chart.

Interindustry Competition

The increasing competition among formerly distinct industries requires a greater consistency in regulation as well as broader coverage. Thrifts and banks are now much more alike, because thrifts now have many bank-like investment powers previously denied to them, and the lifting of interest rate controls has given banks the opportunity to compete with thrifts for retail savings deposits. The differences in portfolio structure between large and small banks is now often more pronounced than that between the small banks and thrifts. In addition, depository institutions have set up affiliates to sell securities, while broker-dealers offer new accounts and services to compete with banks and thrifts. And all institutions, whatever their past successes, are challenged by unregulated firms, innovation, and economic and demographic shifts.

Consider, as an illustration of the current disparities in regulatory policy, the rules governing the emerging competition between banks and thrifts. Banks have a generally broader range of investment alternatives than thrift institutions. But with regard to nonbank activities—those lines of business that must be carried out through a holding company affiliate or a service corporation—the rules for thrift institutions are more permissive. A holding company of only one savings and loan association may engage in any activity; a holding company with multiple savings and loans is restricted to services determined by the Federal Home Loan Bank Board to be related to the main thrift activities. In contrast, bank holding companies, be they unitary or multiple, are confined to a relatively narrow range of nonbank functions. Similarly, a thrift service corporation may engage in a wide variety of activities reasonably related to the operation of the thrift, whereas bank service corporations have only limited powers. These differences arise in part from legislation, but in some cases they reflect asymmetrical interpretations of appropriate activities by the different agencies involved.

As the competition between banks and thrifts intensifies, there will inevitably be justifiable claims of unfair advantage. Even today there is direct competition between banks and thrifts for most kinds of deposits, many types of loans (for example, mortgage, consumer, and student loans, and some types of commercial loans), and the full range of bank holding company and service corporation activities. Congress may address some of the regulatory inconsistencies through new legislation specifying more precisely the powers of holding companies and service corporations; however, the technical knowledge and level of detail required to resolve these issues suggest that they would best be left to the regulatory process. Centralization of regulatory authority therefore seems appropriate as a means of promulgating consistent rules.

With the new asset powers granted in 1982, thrift institutions have begun investing in areas that traditionally were the realm of commercial banks. To take advantage of the expertise of the banks, many thrifts have chosen to enter commercial lending by participating in loans originated by the banks. Consistent regulations for the banks and thrifts enhance the opportunitites to engage in these transactions. Equally important, deposit insurance regulations must apply in an equivalent way to banks and thrifts so that the riskier part of a loan is not shifted to the institution with the less risk-sensitive insurance. One alternative is for the FSLIC and FDIC to develop new insurance regulations in concert. Agency consolidation has obvious advantages in this area.

Mergers and Acquisitions

Mergers of firms regulated by different agencies require that each agency review and approve the combination. Acquisitions by bank holding companies, the most prevalent type of merger, are subject to review by the Federal Reserve, the Department of Justice, and the primary regulator of the acquired firm, although these reviews may be perfunctory. Such transactions have become increasingly common and are forcing regulators to reevaluate the list of permissible lines of business. Electronic funds transfer systems, dispersed loan production offices, and brokered deposits have already broken down many geographic restrictions. The prohibition of mergers is not always an appropriate response; the combinations often yield social benefits such as economies of scale and broader availability of financial services, and the banking industry must undergo a consolidation to remain efficient. Yet when different agencies are involved, there are almost always disagreements, and delay in obtaining the necessary clearances can be costly to the firms involved. Perhaps more important, the public uncertainty created by a dispute among agencies imposes costs on society. Congress and the judiciary are the proper forums for airing and resolving national policy disputes; once decided, however, sound policy requires that the administrative branch of the federal government speak with one voice.[2] With the current consideration of merger policy, it is an opportune time to rationalize the merger approval process.

Regulatory Gaps and Overlaps

Unnecessary problems arise when two or more agencies share responsibility for the safety and soundness of a depository institution. Gaps in regulation can occur if none of the agencies involved asserts sufficient control. This situation may arise because of lack of accountability or because each agency individually is too small to control effectively a large financial institution. Consider the case of bank holding companies. They are regulated, examined, and supervised by the Federal Reserve. Their bank subsidiaries may also be under the jurisdiction of the Federal

2. See Paul M. Horvitz, "Consolidation of the Regulatory Agency Structure: Has the Time for It Come?" *Federal Reserve Bank of Atlanta Economic Review* (December 1982), pp. 50–52.

Reserve (if they are state chartered banks and members of the Federal Reserve System), but they are more likely to be national banks regulated by the Comptroller of the Currency or state banks subject to the controls of state banking agencies and the Federal Deposit Insurance Corporation. Nonbank subsidiaries of the holding company are subject to relatively little regulation. Under these circumstances, companies have attempted to avoid regulation by transferring functions from highly regulated to less regulated subsidiaries. The managers of the firm are treating the company as an integrated whole, while regulators continue to deal with the parts as unrelated entities.

Several bank failures in the 1970s demonstrated the consequences of treating holding company subsidiaries as being independent, although the implications for decentralized regulation are less evident. Three cases suggest the difficulties. Hamilton Bancshares (Tennessee), Beverly Hills Bancorp (California), and Palmer Bancorporation (Florida) were bank holding companies operating in the early 1970s, and each had a national bank as its major subsidiary. Thus their regulation was divided between the Federal Reserve and the Comptroller of the Currency. Nonbank subsidiaries of the three holding companies began making real estate loans, many of which they sold to their bank affiliates. The fact that these transactions took place between affiliates rather than at arm's length was not detected owing to the regulatory arrangement. Although each subsidiary was supervised, transactions between them were not. Many of these loans defaulted when the real estate market slumped in the mid-1970s, and the banks failed.[3] The Federal Reserve has since extended its authority through the holding company to reach the subsidiary institutions. This effort to close a gap in regulation has increased the conflicts between the Federal Reserve and the other bank regulatory agencies. Yet gaps still exist: the impending failure of related Tennessee financial institutions in 1983 was not detected because the various banks and thrifts were separately regulated, and transactions among the units were not detected.

Interagency Conflicts

With the dismantling of traditional industry barriers, it is increasingly likely that bank holding companies will acquire savings institutions and

3. Bernard Shull, "Federal and State Supervision of Bank Holding Companies," in Leonard Lapidus and others, *State and Federal Regulation of Commercial Banks*, vol. 2: *Appraising the System: Significant Activities and Issues, Examination Studies* (Federal Deposit Insurance Corporation, 1980), pp. 350–53.

vice versa. Citicorp, for example, already owns banks in New York and South Dakota and savings and loan associations in California, Illinois, and Florida. Under current law, the parent company falls under the jurisdiction of both the Federal Reserve and the Federal Home Loan Bank Board. As described previously, the range of permitted activities differs substantially between the holding companies of banks and of savings and loans. When firms seek to enter a new field permitted by one agency but not the other, the resulting conflict is usually resolved in favor of the more powerful agency—usually the Federal Reserve.

When two or more agencies assert control and have different interpretations of the law, the conflict leads to delay and extra costs for the firms and the agencies.[4] To take advantage of new powers accorded federal thrift institutions, a mutual savings bank must obtain a federal savings bank charter and thereby come under the authority of the Federal Home Loan Bank Board. Such a change would normally imply a transfer of deposit insurance from the FDIC to the FSLIC, but that transfer could be inequitable without financial compensation. The savings bank would have paid premiums to the FDIC during the period its portfolio was being assembled, yet any assistance costs necessitated by the maturity imbalance of those earlier investment decisions would fall on the FSLIC. The potential liability, however, would be difficult to calculate. This problem forestalled federal chartering between 1980, when the first new powers were granted, and 1982, when a temporary solution was arranged. Now, federal savings banks can continue their FDIC insurance until accepted for insurance by the FSLIC.

In the securities area, a conflict arose between the SEC and the Commodity Futures Trading Commission as soon as the latter agency was formed in 1971. The two agencies each claimed jurisdiction over trading in futures and options contracts for financial instruments. The trading commission based its claim on its authority to regulate commodities exchanges, where the contracts were traded; the SEC asserted that these new instruments were securities and thus fell into its domain. The dispute forestalled the approval of trading in stock index futures and in options on debt securities and foreign currencies. Finally, in late 1981 the two agencies agreed on an arbitrary division of authority that was codified in legislation a year later. But some ambiguity remains, as in the distinction between "broadly based" stock index futures, governed by the commission, and "narrow" ones, governed by the SEC. Both agen-

4. See U.S. General Accounting Office, *The Debate on the Structure of Federal Regulation of Banks* (1977), pp. 23–25.

14

cies continue to regulate options on foreign currencies, depending on whether they are traded on stock exchanges or commodity markets.[5]

The existence of different criteria for identifying problem banks can result in ambiguous signals being sent between the firm and the regulators involved. Remedial action may be delayed because of divergent views among the agencies. A regulator may be reluctant to act unilaterally for fear of inducing banks to change their charters in search of a less stringent agency. Even if prompt steps are taken, achieving coordination among agencies with differing views and objectives requires the costly expense of time and effort. Two examples illustrate the potential for this expense, although agency structure was neither the principal cause of the difficulties of the banks in question nor the major obstacle to their ultimate resolution. The first case concerns the San Francisco National Bank, which encountered severe financial difficulties in 1964. The Comptroller of the Currency was aware of the bank's condition and took steps to remedy the problems, but it did not inform the Federal Reserve or the FDIC of what it had found. The bank was placed in receivership the next year, but that step came only after substantial and perhaps costly delay. A congressional subcommittee concluded that the case was "a clear illustration of the breakdown of liaison and lack of cooperation among the banking agencies."[6]

Second, in 1974, the losses suffered by the Franklin National Bank on foreign exchange contracts threatened its existence. The Comptroller of the Currency had the authority to close the bank but sought a merger partner instead. While this search took place, uninsured depositors started a run on the bank that required substantial advances from the Federal Reserve System. Because there was insufficient collateral for these advances, the FDIC was asked to guarantee them, which it was reluctant to do without assurances from the Comptroller of the Currency that the problem would be addressed quickly. The problem was resolved, but, again, only after considerable delay. The FDIC lost nothing and creditors were ultimately repaid, but swifter action might have preserved some of the bank's assets for shareholders. It was not until late 1983 that the Comptroller of the Currency agreed to "invite" the FDIC to examine problem national banks, never acknowledging the right of

---

5. Commodity Futures Trading Commission, *Annual Report 1982* (Government Printing Office, 1983), pp. 23–24.

6. *Investigation into Federally Insured Banks,* Committee Print, Senate Committee on Government Operations, 89 Cong. 2 sess. (GPO, 1966), pp. 9–10; Walter A. Varvel, "FDIC Policy Toward Bank Failures," *Economic Review,* vol. 62 (September–October 1976), pp. 6–7.

the FDIC to do so on its own authority. The common lesson of these two cases is that when necessary measures are postponed, problems become difficult—and perhaps more expensive—to correct.[7]

Differing Goals

Competing regulatory objectives create problems even when the issue is not a failing bank. The primary goals of the three principal federal bank regulators are different and not necessarily consistent: for the Comptroller of the Currency, it is to maintain the banking system; for the Federal Reserve, it is to stabilize the money supply; and for the FDIC, it is to preserve the insurance fund. At the same time, the regulators are also charged with maintaining competition, fostering innovation, and meeting the needs of the community; these activities, which involve risk taking and the possibility of failure, can clash with the regulators' primary goals.[8]

In the case of bank regulation, the Federal Reserve and FDIC exert a conservative influence, while the chartering authority (the Comptroller of the Currency or the state) encourages development and growth. Because the bank chartering authority is independent of the Federal Reserve and FDIC, it need not defer to those agencies' concerns about risky behavior on the part of banks. On the other hand, the chartering authority lacks recourse if the Federal Reserve uses its holding company controls or the FDIC uses its insurance regulations to restrict bank activity unduly. There is no reason to expect that the policy balance achieved in this manner is the correct one. There is thus a continuing tension within the agencies as they pursue their different ends.

One of the most serious conflicts occurred during the mid-1960s between the Comptroller of the Currency and the other federal regulators. The Comptroller had ruled that national banks could enter a number of new lines of business under that part of the Banking Act providing for "incidental powers." Among the new lines were acceptance of corporate savings deposits, purchase of corporate stock, and underwriting of municipal revenue bonds. The Comptroller also permitted banks to use accounting definitions that effectively relaxed certain loan and capital restrictions. The Federal Reserve, which also has

---

7. Andrew S. Carron, "Financial Crises: Recent Experience in U.S. and International Markets," *Brookings Papers on Economic Activity, 2:1982*, pp. 398–400; GAO, *Federal Regulation of Banks*, pp. 15–19.

8. Stanley C. Silverberg, "Bank Supervision and Competitive Laxity," *The Magazine of Bank Administration*, vol. 52 (January 1976), pp. 20–21.

authority over national banks, objected to many of these grants of authority. In the course of the dispute, the Comptroller withheld examination reports from the FDIC, which may have impaired the insurance agency's ability to address the problems of the San Francisco National Bank.[9] During the course of the dispute, which lasted several years, the national banks were uncertain about what activities were legal, and state chartered banks felt they were being unfairly treated.

Most examples of regulatory disarray involve commercial banks, because there is almost no overlapping regulation of a given thrift institution, credit union, securities dealer, or commodity broker. (There have been conflicts between the Securities and Exchange Commission and the Commodity Futures Trading Commission over futures and options on financial instruments, but the divisions of responsibility between these agencies are mostly clear.) For the Federal Home Loan Bank Board, the National Credit Union Administration, the SEC, and the Commodity Futures Trading Commission, policy debates are internal. A decision is made on the desired trade-off between safety and competition, and all policies are set to attain that balance. If the decisions of a single agency are incompatible with overall government policy, they can be corrected through legislative or judicial means. It is inherently more difficult to develop and implement a consistent policy when instructions must be given separately to two or more agencies, each of which will react to the others' shifts in rules and procedures.

Operating Cost Savings

One of the appealing aspects of regulatory consolidation is the apparent promise of reduced administrative expense. For example, the major bank regulatory agencies developed their approaches to examinations independently and maintain separate schools for the training of examiners.[10] Duplication also exists in the agencies' computer systems and data bases.[11] However, the largest direct expenses associated with financial regulation are the payments made to weak institutions and to depositors of failed institutions. In 1981, such payments accounted for more than

9. Howard H. Hackley, "Our Baffling Banking System," *Virginia Law Review,* vol. 52 (May 1966), pp. 598–632. See also the reply in Carter H. Golembe, "Our Remarkable Banking System," *Virginia Law Review Annual Index,* vol. 53 (1967), pp. 1100–07.

10. "Toward a More Responsive Regulatory Structure," in *Financial Institutions Act, 1973,* Hearings before the Subcommittee on Financial Institutions, Senate Committee on Banking, Housing, and Urban Affairs, 93 Cong. 2 sess. (GPO, 1974), pp. 127–207.

11. GAO, *Federal Supervision of State and National Banks* (GPO, 1977), pp. 11-4–11-6.

85 percent of FHLBB expenses, 85 percent of FDIC expenses, and 82 percent of NCUA expenses.[12] These payments are a function of the operating performance of insured firms and would not be affected by the consolidation of the agencies.

The examination of regulated institutions accounts for most of the remaining agency expenses. However, the agencies have tried to avoid duplicate or inconsistent examinations. For example, the Comptroller of the Currency, the Federal Reserve, and the FDIC have divided the responsibilities among themselves for federally insured banks; the Federal Reserve and the FDIC have, in turn, arranged with many states to alternate their examinations of state chartered banks and to accept each other's reports. For its part, the FHLBB's Office of Examination and Supervision conducts both regulatory and insurance examinations and conducts joint examinations with state agencies. Thus the extent of duplication is probably small, as are the agencies' remaining administrative costs (table 2). The upper bound for potential savings, equal to the overhead expenses of the agencies, amounts to only 0.001 to 0.018 percent of assets. Of course, the actual cost savings would be even smaller. At much less than one-half of one basis point (before tax), the reduction in operating costs would have no measurable effect on returns to depositors, borrowing costs, or industry profitability.

There are some duplicate reporting requirements that could be avoided. National banks with international operations, for example, must report both to the Federal Reserve (Edge Act offices) and to the Comptroller of the Currency (foreign branches). In some cases, the definitions used by the agencies may differ; they have only recently established common criteria for "nonperforming loans." These overlaps can easily be corrected, however; the Federal Financial Institutions Examination Council has already solved many of them. It must be concluded that consolidation offers little potential for operating cost savings.

The large share of expenses devoted to assistance suggests there may be savings obtainable from a consolidation of the deposit insurance funds. When a resource such as an insurance fund reserve is subject to random demands, the principle of "economies of massed reserves" may apply. At a larger size, it is easier to meet fluctuations in demand: the greater the number of firms that are served, the more likely it is that random claims will occur at a steady and predictable rate. Thrift and

12. Federal Home Loan Bank Board, *1981 Annual Report*, pp. 93–94; FDIC, *1981 Annual Report*, vol. 1, p. 28; National Credit Union Share Insurance Fund, *Annual Financial Report: Fiscal Year 1981*, p. 23.

Table 2. *Operating Expenses of the Bank Regulatory Agencies, 1982*
Millions of dollars, except where otherwise noted

Expense	Federal Reserve	Office of the Comptroller of the Currency	Federal Deposit Insurance Corporation	Federal Home Loan Bank Board	National Credit Union Administration
Regulatory expenses	n.a.	144.5	999.8	981.3	127.1
Minus: Assistance to failing institutions	0.0	0.0	815.7	865.3	80.4
Supervision and examination expense	127.0	130.7	86.1	37.3	19.8
Effect of financial transactions	n.a.	0.0	54.2	50.5	13.6
Equals: Potential duplicated expenses	n.a.	13.9	43.8	28.2	13.3
As share of expenses (percent)	n.a.	9.6	4.4	2.9	10.5
As share of industry assets (percent)	n.a.	0.001	0.007	0.004	0.018
Addendum Industry assets	333,095	1,069,983	623,894	692,663	75,638

Source: Author's estimates based on Board of Governors of the Federal Reserve System, *69th Annual Report 1982*; Federal Deposit Insurance Corporation, *1982 Annual Report*; *Federal Home Loan Bank Board Journal: Annual Report 1982*, vol. 16 (April 1983); National Credit Union Administration, *1982 Annual Report*; NCUA, Central Liquidity Facility, *Annual Financial Report, Fiscal Year 1982*; National Credit Union Share Insurance Fund, *Annual Financial Report, Fiscal Year 1982*; FDIC, *1982 Statistics on Banking*, p. 19; *The Budget of the United States Government, Fiscal Year 1983*.
n.a. Not available.

bank claims have a lower correlation between industries than within industries, implying a lower variance for a combined fund than for separate funds. Thus the balance tips in favor of consolidation.

It should be noted that the size of the insurance funds has not been determined actuarially. In the event a fund is exhausted, an implicit federal promise exists to fulfill the fund's obligations. There is thus no basis for assuming that a consolidated fund should bear a lower (or higher) relationship to deposits than the funds do separately.

State-Federal Conflicts

The confusion and inconsistency at the federal level should not obscure the fact that conflicts often arise between state and federal bank regulators, especially over banks or thrift institutions that are state chartered and federally insured. State regulators may be less restrictive than their federal counterparts, because the cost of bank failure is largely transferred to the federal deposit insurance agency. The FDIC and the Federal Home Loan Bank Board (through its Federal Savings and Loan

Insurance Corporation) therefore attempt to use insurance regulations to control more broadly the activities of state chartered institutions. Such a case developed recently when the California legislature expanded the investment authority it grants to state chartered savings and loan associations. To counter the California action, which it regarded as too risky, the FHLBB proposed a rule to deny FSLIC deposit insurance to institutions that engage in certain of the newly approved activities, notably real estate development.[13] Unless California can show that this rule exceeds FHLBB authority, state institutions will be compelled to accede. Federal deposit insurance is a necessity for these firms, and thus the deposit insurance agencies have great leverage over state regulators. The principle of dual banking can survive only to the extent that the states adhere to the general guidelines set down by the federal agencies.

The Case against Consolidation

There are four main arguments against consolidation. Chief among these is the fact that the existing system has worked reasonably well. The next two arguments are based on the diversity and decentralization of the system: giving the industry a choice of regulators encourages the agencies to be responsive to industry needs (argument two), and having several regulators share authority for a single firm keeps the agencies from getting too close to the industry (argument three). The fourth argument is that differences between banks and thrifts outweigh the similarities, and thus specialized regulation is still called for. These arguments have been made by different groups at different times, and they are not necessarily consistent with each other.

Performance of the Old System

It is difficult to argue that the regulatory agency system in place for the last fifty years has seriously impeded the development of the financial services industry. In general, stability has been maintained; although bank failures have reached record high levels, the causes have little or nothing to do with regulatory structure. The consolidation issue turns, instead, on whether the financial sector has changed sufficiently to invalidate past experience as a guide to the future.

---

13. "Reserve Requirements and Policies Relating to Insurance of Accounts of *De Novo* Institutions," FHLBB news release, November 3, 1983.

Some have suggested that it may be possible to minimize the problems of gaps and overlaps in regulation while maintaining multiple agencies. Indeed, several attempts have been made to coordinate the activities of the federal regulators: in 1938, the three federal bank regulatory agencies developed common standards for classifying bank assets and appraising securities; from 1952 to 1960 a committee coordinated the regulators' standards and activities; the Interagency Coordinating Committee on Bank Regulation, formed in 1965, and more recently the Federal Financial Institutions Examination Council, have tried to resolve problems arising between the Comptroller of the Currency and other agencies. The Depository Institutions Deregulation Committee is an interagency group created in 1980 to manage the removal of deposit interest rate ceilings.

Competition among Regulators

One of the advantages seen in the current system is the check on the power of the regulatory agencies. Today a depository institution may choose among several different types of state and federal charters; with each goes a different primary regulator, and there is a choice of insurer as well. Now that the distinctions between banks and thrifts have been lessened, the options are even wider. In addition to the long-standing alternatives among the three federal bank regulators, a commercial bank might now seek to operate as a federal savings bank under the Federal Home Loan Bank Board. Presumably, if one regulatory body is more stringent, less innovative, or more cumbersome than the others, firms under its jurisdiction will seek to change their charters, and newly organized firms will not choose to come under that regulator. Thus the agencies compete to retain their jurisdiction by offering operating conditions that are most attractive from the point of view of the firms. Some have called this behavior "competition in laxity."[14]

Competition among the regulators is thought to take place along several dimensions. Regulators may disagree in their views of the most desirable market structure for financial institutions and may therefore differ on proposed mergers, branches, or holding companies. An institution can arrange a transaction so as to come under the jurisdiction of the more lenient regulator. Over the years, new authorities have been

14. Silverberg, "Bank Supervision"; and Thomas Mayer, James S. Duesenberry, and Robert Z. Aliber, eds., *Money, Banking and the Economy* (W. W. Norton, 1981), pp. 210–12.

granted to banks and thrifts through statutory changes by Congress and also through new interpretations of existing law by the regulators. It is in the granting of asset, liability, and service powers that regulators have had the greatest scope. In the 1960s the Comptroller of the Currency took a more liberal view of banking law than other federal regulators, and a number of banks, including the Chase Manhattan Bank, switched to national bank charters to take advantage of the new powers. State chartered thrift institutions in New England developed NOW accounts and were permitted to offer them in the early 1970s, while a federal prohibition on the practice remained in effect. This permitted the testing of an innovation in a limited market to demonstrate its feasibility, a practice that probably would not have been possible with a single national regulator. A third example can be seen in the real estate lending powers of commercial banks. Although national banks were restricted in this area, many state statutes were silent, thus permitting state banks to experiment. After the practice proved viable, national banks were granted many of the same powers.

Regulatory Capture

One common result of government regulation is that regulatory agencies eventually come to serve the interests of the industry instead of the public. That is because the agency has daily contact with firms in the industry and measures its own success in terms of the health of the regulated. Unfortunately, profitability can be the result of regulated prices set too high, the propping up of inefficient firms, or the exclusion of competitive firms from the market. This identification of the regulator with the regulated is termed "regulatory capture."

Advocates of the current structure believe that shared supervision, such as the division of insurance and supervisory functions among two or more agencies in the case of most depository institutions, reduces the likelihood of agency capture. Hence some view multiple levels of control as a benefit of the current structure.

Specialized Institutions

The banking, thrift, credit union, and securities sectors developed separately with specialized regulators. Despite the innovations of recent years, firms and agencies today still look quite different. Although the variation will fade with time as institutions exercise their increased flexibility, the existing structure of the firms and practices of the agencies

22

may initially be difficult to reconcile. Thrifts do not want to be put under a bank regulator; banks doing securities business want to minimize SEC intervention; state chartered institutions resent the intrusion of federal agencies; and national banks would prefer that only the Comptroller of the Currency and not the Federal Reserve or the FDIC monitor their operations.

The savings and loan industry has maintained that specialized regulation is necessary to support its social mission of providing housing finance; therefore it opposes consolidation of the Federal Home Loan Bank Board or FSLIC with one or another of the federal bank regulators.[15] In part, the justification for this view rests on the very different structure and condition of banks and thrifts today; there would have to be a transition period before thrifts and banks could be treated alike. But a stronger assertion is put forward by both the thrift industry and the Bank Board, namely, that this specialized function of thrifts should continue. A related concern is that after a merger of two agencies, the traditional membership of the surviving agency may be favored, whether it be national banks over state banks, banks over thrifts, stock institutions over mutual firms, or large over small.

The particular history of depository institutions has made each set of institutions especially vulnerable to a different type of risk.[16] Is it possible to design a single regulatory system to deal equitably with all institutions under a consolidated agency? Expansion of portfolio powers will permit some convergence, but the nature of the institutions indicates that some distinctions will persist. For instance, the traditional thrift portfolio's exposure to interest rate risk is well known. New asset powers, including alternative mortgage instruments, can ameliorate this problem. Yet thrifts will remain subject to interest rate swings for many years and may even choose to continue long-term portfolio lending. Banks are unlikely ever to become as sensitive to rates, but they have their own problem—credit risk. Another difference between banks and thrifts is that private capital provides a larger buffer for the banks' insurance fund than in the thrift industry, while a smaller share of total deposits is covered by federal deposit insurance. Banks and thrifts have different capital requirements. Moreover, the accounting standards for

15. Edwin J. Gray, "Shaping the Modern Home Mortgage Lending and Depository Institution for the Long-Term Future: Realities and Critical Questions," speech delivered at the 91st annual convention of the U.S. League of Savings Institutions, November 15, 1983.

16. A detailed discussion of risk can be found in FHLBB, *Agenda for Reform: A Report on Deposit Insurance to the Congress from the Federal Home Loan Bank Board* (The Board, 1983).

each industry differ—banks must follow "generally accepted" account-ing principles while most thrifts are permitted to use the more permis-sive "regulatory" accounting principles. In addition, the maturity dis-crepancy between thrift assets and liabilities means that the market value of assets (and therefore net worth) will diverge more widely from book value.

The credit unions are not affected by interest rates as much as the savings institutions are, because their portfolios are more closely matched. And because they lend to members whose earnings and credit histories are well known, the exposure to default risk is less than banks'. But credit unions, the smallest of the depository institutions, are not diversified sufficiently to avoid unsystematic risks. Their managements may be inexperienced, serve only part-time, and be called upon to undertake diverse tasks; and thus the possibility for mistakes or poor performance (management risk) is perhaps their greatest concern.

Recommendations

The major arguments for consolidation are the gaps and conflicts in current regulation, inconsistencies in powers and authorities, and the difficulties in providing assistance to failing banks. The most substantive case in favor of the present system argues that it leads to beneficial competition among regulators, avoids regulatory capture, supports the virtues of specialization, and aids in the control of monetary policy.

The Arguments Assessed

The savings and loan industry is a useful counterexample to the notion that competition in regulation is essential to innovation. Even though it is under the control of a single federal agency, the industry has been as progressive as the banking sector.[17] Decentralized review of merger applications, permissive funds transfer regulations, and a pro-gram for long-term advances have all arisen under the monolithic structure of savings and loan regulation.

Moreover, the new regulatory environment reduces the importance of the regulatory agency in controlling the development of the industry. Statutory limitations are now less stringent and thus leave the agency

17. See GAO, *Federal Regulation of Banks*, pp. 41–43; and *Study on Federal Regula-tion: Regulatory Organization*, Senate Committee on Government Affairs, 95 Cong. 1 sess. (GPO, 1977), vol. 5, pp. 224–26.

fewer issues to be decided. Distinctions between the banking and thrift industries are fewer, reducing the potential differences in regulatory practice. Perhaps most important, a large and highly developed non-depository financial sector exists to provide a competitive check on excessive regulation. Securities firms and mutual funds offer an array of investment products similar to bank and thrift deposits. Households can borrow through finance companies and mortgage bankers as well as from depository institutions. Corporations can tap the capital markets directly.

Regulatory capture can take place only when the regulatory agency has the ability to provide benefits and protections to the firms under its aegis; competition from unregulated firms can reduce or eliminate these advantages. In earlier times, for example, the Federal Home Loan Bank Board may have taken actions to shield savings and loan associations from market forces. But today, even though the Bank Board is sole regulator for federal savings associations, it could do little to raise profitability or restrict competition because of the challenges from outside the industry. While the banks might be brought under common regulatory control in a new organizational plan, there would still be myriad securities brokers, mutual funds, and others able to compete unfettered.

Although the issue of industry specialization is beyond the scope of this paper, two points can be made. First, with the clear intention that thrifts would compete with commercial banks, Congress enacted legislation in 1980 and 1982 that permitted thrift institutions to invest in assets and accept liabilities previously restricted to commercial banks. Second, it is not axiomatic that a consolidated bank-thrift regulator would be incapable of carrying out the government's housing finance policy. Nor does specialization resolve the problem of discriminatory treatment. The potential for discrimination exists even today: the FDIC insures the largest financial institutions, but its average member is smaller than the average FSLIC-insured savings and loan association; both the FDIC and FSLIC insure stock and mutual, large and small, federal and state firms.

It is difficult to achieve uniform treatment when different agencies are setting the rules for similar activities. The difficulty has been that, being independent, each agency feels bound to assert its statutory authority and responsibility. Coordination will become increasingly difficult as the financial services industries evolve toward one another and share numerous areas of interaction. This convergence of industry structures undermines the logic of specialized regulation and enhances the need for a consolidated agency; it makes regulation by function appropriate for

25

the financial system now evolving. Finally, organizational efficiency and the minimization of transactions costs argue for consolidation. Statutory change, whether involving consolidation of the agencies or merely a redefinition of powers, is indicated.

Recommended Structure

Rationalization should begin with the creation of a single primary bank regulator that would assume all the powers of the Comptroller of the Currency and the FDIC and those of the Federal Reserve with respect to state member banks. In addition, the new agency would have jurisdiction over those holding companies whose lead institution is a bank. Creation of this regulator would eliminate substantial overlaps of authority and would permit consolidation of the regional offices of the Comptroller of the Currency and the FDIC. Banks could retain the option of chartering under federal or state law, but state chartered banks that sought federal deposit insurance would be subject to appropriate controls by the federal regulator, which could also delegate examination responsibilities to state regulators. This model for banks is essentially similar to the current arrangement for thrifts. Although this structure might appear to diminish the importance and flexibility of state chartering, the reality is that federal regulators have already usurped the substance of state authority through the control of conditions for deposit insurance and liquidity support.

The new federal banking regulator should be independent, not part of any other government agency. It should be governed by presidential appointees so that it would have the necessary amount of autonomy and authority while still being sensitive to the broad concerns of the executive branch. Again, the model of the Federal Home Loan Bank Board is instructive.

The reorganization just described would bring bank regulation to the same degree of rationalization as thrift regulation. Further consolidation would involve substantial shifts of jurisdiction and would probably encounter great political opposition, but the case for it is strong, even if it cannot be easily or quickly accomplished. Despite broad support for the continued existence of specialized housing lenders, most thrifts will compete with banks in many lines of business, and some thrifts will choose to act like banks; moreover, many financial market concerns transcend institutional boundaries. These trends argue for common regulation. One means of achieving uniform regulation would be coordination of bank and thrift regulators, but attempts at such coordination have generally failed. Inevitably, the only practical way of resolving the increasing number of disputes that will come about is to bring thrifts and banks under the same regulatory agency.

As for the Federal Reserve's interest in bank regulation, the central bank already has the authority to adjust reserve requirements and terms for discount window borrowing for all banks and thrifts. In addition, as the central bank, the Federal Reserve must have the final authority for certain matters of overriding importance to the financial system and therefore must have access to detailed and timely information on the liquidity and soundness of individual institutions. But the Federal Reserve's routine regulatory powers should be transferred away; it does not have to be a primary regulator, supervisor, or deposit insurer to conduct its activities effectively.

Conclusion

The debates on reform of the financial regulatory structure are striking in two respects. One is the sheer number of studies, panels, commissions, and recommendations that have been forthcoming in a nearly continuous stream since the early years of regulation in this century (see appendix B), which suggests widespread agreement on the need for reform. The recommendations flowing out of these efforts have usually envisioned a moderate-to-substantial consolidation of the agencies. The other remarkable feature has been the repetitiveness of the arguments on all sides of the issue; this stalemate in argumentation leads one to conclude that the time for study has passed. A decision on whether and how to reorganize the system must now be made on the basis of available information.

The weight of evidence indicates that the current patchwork arrangement has been adequate for an era of strict industry regulation. Although a case for rationalization has always existed, it has not been compelling until now because regulatory shortcomings have been offset by some modest advantages of diversity. But the financial industry's future will be different and unpredictable. The emerging economic environment demands corresponding changes in the regulatory structure. Existing weaknesses in the regulatory scheme, such as the coordination problem in interindustry matters, will come under increasing pressure, while the importance of the system's strength—its openness to diversity—will fade as the unregulated market provides the spark of innovation.

There needs now to be a single coherent policy toward financial institutions. If the policy is too rigid, then Congress or the administration can propose changes in the governing statutes or seek modifications in regulatory practice through oversight and appointment. As part of this policy, federal regulation of depository institutions should be consolidated and centralized, and the more so the better. But this consolidation should proceed in tandem with the resolution of a broader issue— competition between depository institutions, which are the traditional objects of regulation, and other firms, which are not similarly controlled. To resolve this issue, Congress must redefine "banking" and permitted activities of bank holding companies. Redefinition will bring some activities under bank regulation for the first time, even as banks begin to engage in new, unregulated activities themselves; the more coherent industry that results from this process will require a more coherent regulatory system. Regulatory change thus must proceed in concert with structural reform of the industry.

Historical Background to Regulation

GOVERNMENT regulation of financial institutions dates from the early years of our nation's history, but the practice of this intervention has not been continuous nor has its philosophy been consistent.

Depository Institutions

Until the Civil War, private banks and many nonfinancial corporations had to obtain charters from state legislatures. Some banks were owned, in whole or in part, by the state governments; the states, in their capacity as shareholders, demanded periodic reports on the condition of these banks, and this practice seems to have been the precursor of bank examination and regulation. Formal state supervision accompanied the development of deposit insurance systems in many states during the mid-nineteenth century. Beginning in 1838, New York law allowed for chartered banks covered by the state's insurance plan and for uninsured "free banks," which could be established with minimal restrictions.[18]

Banks

Federal involvement in the financial industry began with the federally chartered Banks of the United States, which served as central banks from 1791 to 1836 (with a hiatus from 1811 to 1816). Federal intervention in the regulation of state banks began in 1819, when the House of Representatives included state banks in its investigation of the Second Bank of the United States.[19] There was no federal role in banking after 1836, when the charter of the Second Bank expired, until the Civil War, by which time the reliance on state banks for currency issue and on state regulation for maintaining confidence in the financial system proved insufficient. This was the era of "wildcat banking," when banks located their offices

18. Golembe, "Our Remarkable Banking System," p. 1096.
19. Ross M. Robertson, *The Comptroller and Bank Supervision: A Historical Appraisal* (Office of the Comptroller of the Currency, 1968), pp. 24–27.

"where only the wildcats lived" to hinder redemption of bank notes as well as to deter close scrutiny of operations.[20]

The Office of the Comptroller of the Currency. The National Currency Act, passed in 1863, was concerned mainly with currency stability and federal debt management, but it also established the chartering of privately owned national banks.[21] By providing a federal license, this law gave banks a means of circumventing the political obstacles to forming new banks in some states. These federally chartered banks could issue national bank notes, which were a precursor of the nationwide payments system and a means of controlling the national supply of currency. The Office of the Comptroller of the Currency was a new office established in the Treasury Department to administer the provisions of the act.

Banks with state charters were reluctant to adopt national charters, which carried with them the prospect of national control, until Congress imposed a prohibitive tax on the issue of notes by state banks (the notes were a mechanism used to make loans). Becuse deposits in state chartered banks were increasingly replacing notes, however, this measure was only partially successful in encouraging national charters and laid the foundations of the "dual" (state-federal) banking system that persists to this day. The number of state banks declined from 1,089 in 1864 to 325 in 1870 but then rose to 3,773 in 1892, surpassing the number of national banks.[22] Both state agencies and the Comptroller of the Currency developed systems of bank supervision and made rules for the formation of branch offices.

The Federal Reserve System. The reforms implemented during the Civil War established a uniform national currency but failed to stabilize the banking system. Depositors repeatedly started runs on banks thought to be in trouble, in so doing creating the outcome that was feared. Even solvent, well-managed banks had no way of meeting massive withdrawals. These bank crises, especially the Panic of 1907, caused rapid deflation in the economy. The Federal Reserve Act of 1913, the next piece of bank regulatory legislation, was intended to stem these repeated monetary crises. It created a nationwide system of check clearing,

---

20. The development of banking regulation is discussed in detail elsewhere. See, for example, F. Ward McCarthy, Jr., "The Evolution of the Bank Regulatory Structure: A Reappraisal," *Federal Reserve Bank of Richmond Economic Review,* vol. 70 (March–April 1984), pp. 3–21; Tim S. Campbell, *Financial Institutions, Markets, and Economic Activity* (McGraw-Hill, 1982), pp. 414–92; and Lawrence S. Ritter and William L. Silber, *Principles of Money, Banking, and Financial Markets* (Basic Books, 1980), pp. 96–113.

21. 12 Stat. 665. Revisions made the following year were titled the National Bank Act of 1864, 13 Stat. 99.

22. GAO, *Federal Supervision of State and National Banks,* pp. 1-8-1-10.

consolidated required reserves in the central bank, and set up a mechanism for lending to banks.[23] Because national banks were required to join the Federal Reserve System, the agency was granted authority with the Comptroller of the Currency to examine these banks. State chartered banks could, at their option, also join the Federal Reserve System. In practice, the Comptroller of the Currency remained the primary regulator of national banks, the Federal Reserve became the primary regulator of state member (that is, Federal Reserve member) banks, and the states retained primary jurisdiction over state nonmember banks.

The most important of the Federal Reserve's regulatory powers was granted by the Bank Holding Company Act of 1956, under which it has primary jurisdiction over bank holding companies whether or not the consitituent banks are Federal Reserve members. Through the holding company, the Federal Reserve monitors and regulates the investment powers of the subsidiary banks and rules on proposed acquisitions by holding companies or their banks.

A large part of the Federal Reserve's income is interest on loans and securities and profits on open market operations; however, the bulk of funds from those sources is turned back to the Treasury. Examination fees help to defray regulatory expenses.

The Federal Deposit Insurance Corporation. The crisis of the Great Depression forced a fundamental change in bank regulation. Laws passed during 1932–34 completed the structure of the financial services industry and its regulatory agencies that exists today. As the depression hit, depositors faced an incentive to start bank runs, because there was a potentially high cost associated with forbearance and virtually no cost with a precipitate withdrawal of funds. From 1928 to 1933 more than 9,000 banks went under;[24] although monetary contraction was the principal cause, these failures were blamed on unsound banking practices and inadequate regulation. Because the Federal Reserve System had failed to support the banking system in this crisis, government controls became much stricter, and Congress created a new regulatory mechanism to protect depositors directly rather than through support of the depository institution: the Federal Deposit Insurance Corporation (FDIC), first of the insurance funds.

Established under the Banking Act of 1933 by an amendment to the Federal Reserve Act of 1913, the FDIC was organized under its own governing authority, a three-member board composed of the Comptrol-

23. 38 Stat. 251.
24. U.S. Bureau of the Census, *Historical Statistics of the United States: Colonial Times to 1970* (GPO, 1975), pt. 2, p. 1038.

ler of the Currency and two presidential appointees, one of whom was to serve as chairman and chief executive officer.[25] This measure of independence from the Comptroller of the Currency and the Federal Reserve was an artifact of the already fragmented nature of the federal banking regulatory apparatus. From its inception in 1863, the Comptroller of the Currency had been in charge of the chartering, regulation, and supervision of national banks; with the exception of chartering, the Federal Reserve had since 1913 performed these functions for state member banks. In contrast, deposit insurance was intended not for a segment of the industry but for all banks: national and state member banks and state nonmember banks that previously were exempt from federal regulation. If the FDIC were to be made part of one of the two existing federal regulatory agencies, state nonmember banks feared that they would thereby fall into the orbit of federal regulation beyond that required to obtain insurance. Likewise, institutions already under the control of one of the two federal regulators feared that if the FDIC were placed in the hands of the other federal regulator, they would receive less favorable treatment than if the FDIC were independent. So the FDIC was established as an independent agency to avoid these political concerns.

Although a provision of the 1933 act required all insured banks to become members of the Federal Reserve by 1936, thereby eliminating the FDIC's supervisory role, state banking interests ultimately prevailed: the Banking Act of 1935 extended the deadline to 1941, and in 1939 the membership requirement was repealed.[26] The structure as settled upon in 1939 gave new and smaller banks the same high credit standing in the eyes of depositors as the larger and older institutions, and so encouraged the proliferation of bank ownership. The responsibility for supervision of state nonmember banks rests clearly with the FDIC, though this jurisdiction is shared with state banking authorities. The power to close a bank remains with the chartering body—the Comptroller of the Currency in the case of national banks and the state authorities in the case of state member and nonmember banks. The Banking Act of 1935 consolidated the insurance funds for mutual savings banks into the FDIC fund.

Before the Great Depression, some banks had encouraged customers to purchase stock in troubled companies to protect the banks' loans to those companies. When the wave of business failures came, both banks and shareholders lost. The Glass-Steagall Act, adopted as a section of the 1933 legislation, thus provides for the separation of commercial and

25. 48 Stat. 168.
26. "Toward a More Responsive Regulatory Structure," pp. 27–207.

investment banking businesses. Since the passage of Glass-Steagall, member banks that engage in commercial banking—accepting deposits or making loans to commercial enterprises—cannot trade or underwrite corporate securities, except as trustees or as agents.

Bank Holding Companies

The holding company is the means by which banks—more closely regulated than nonbank intermediaries and nonfinancial corporations—have evaded some controls.[27] Banks have used holding companies to circumvent interstate and intrastate branching restrictions, to raise and invest funds unencumbered by capital and interest rate restrictions, and to minimize tax liability. The holding company has therefore become the preferred form of organization for most banks. Such companies hold more than one-third of the nation's 14,500 banks and account for three-fourths of domestic commercial bank deposits.[28]

Legislation beginning with the Banking Act of 1933 and continuing with the Bank Holding Company Act of 1956 and its 1970 amendments today requires the Federal Reserve to supervise all bank holding companies and prohibits holding companies from owning stock in nonbanking entities that fail a public benefits test or are not "closely related to the business of banking."[29] The 1956 legislation also explicitly recognized the rights of states to regulate the activities of holding companies and their affiliates and subsidiaries. In particular, the Douglas amendment prohibited holding companies from acquiring banks in states other than the one in which the lead bank was located unless permitted by state law. The amendment permitted many multistate holding companies to continue operating, but it halted their further expansion outside their home states. The system of holding company regulation thus involves the regulators of the constituent banks and of their nonbank subsidiaries plus the Federal Reserve as regulator of holding companies and of their nonbank subsidiaries. A bank holding company that owns a national

27. The term *nonbank* refers to financial institutions other than commercial banks, such as savings and loan associations, savings banks, credit unions, finance companies, securities firms, investment companies, and insurance companies.

28. Robert A. Eisenbeis, "Bank Holding Companies and Public Policy," in George J. Benston, ed., *Financial Services: The Changing Institutions and Government Policy* (Prentice-Hall, 1983), pp. 127–28.

29. Bank Holding Company Act of 1956, 70 Stat. 133; and Bank Holding Company Amendments of 1970, 84 Stat. 1760. A bank holding company was originally defined as a corporation owning a majority interest in a bank. The definition was subsequently expanded to include all corporations with effective control over a bank.

bank and a state nonmember bank is therefore regulated by the Federal Reserve, the Comptroller of the Currency, the FDIC, and the state.

In recent years, bank holding companies have sought broader powers for their nonbank subsidiaries. Citing concerns about the stability of the financial system and the increase in market concentration, the Federal Reserve generally has been reluctant to permit new activities and sees the proposed powers as involving riskier investments that could imperil the affiliated banks. State regulators see multistate holding companies as competitive threats to banks operating in a single state and subject only to the rules of that state. For their part, the large bank holding companies view such objections as impediments to operating efficiencies and competitive equality with nonbank enterprises such as insurance companies, securities dealers, and financial conglomerates. The example of savings and loan associations, which possess broader holding company authority and recently have been granted commercial lending powers, is also put forward by the bankers in their case for deregulation.

Thrift Institutions

Savings and loan associations and mutual savings banks operated exclusively under state regulation until most of the federal regulation of commercial banks was already in place. Savings and loan associations were devastated by the Great Depression: their assets had consisted largely of short-term mortgage loans, and when those came due, many borrowers defaulted. Perhaps because the thrift industry was relatively small or as a result of the experience with banks, federal regulation of thrifts has been centralized from the start through three laws. The Federal Home Loan Bank Act of 1932 provided a credit reserve for thrift institutions by setting up twelve federal home loan banks capitalized by member institutions and the U.S. Treasury and authorized to lend limited amounts without collateral.[30] The 1932 act established the Federal Home Loan Bank Board (FHLBB), made up of three presidential appointees, and charged it with regulating and supervising the twelve home loan banks. The Home Owners Loan Act of 1933 gave to the FHLBB responsibility for chartering, regulating, and supervising federally chartered savings and loan associations.[31]

---

30. 47 Stat. 725.

31. 48 Stat. 128. This law also authorized the FHLBB to "promote" the organization of savings and loan associations, and money was appropriated to the board for that purpose. That provision remains, but in 1956 the board announced in a letter that it was formally discontinuing its promotional activities. The letter noted that the original need for the

Because thrift institutions competed with banks for deposits, it was felt necessary to provide a comparable form of deposit insurance. Thus, in 1934, title IV of the National Housing Act established the Federal Savings and Loan Insurance Corporation (FSLIC) to insure the accounts of all federally chartered savings and loan associations.[32] Control and management of the FSLIC were vested in the members of the Federal Home Loan Bank Board, who were named trustees of the insurance agency. State chartered institutions, including those not part of the Federal Home Loan Bank System, were eligible for FSLIC insurance; in 1935 mutual savings banks, which were less closely linked to housing finance, were made eligible for FDIC insurance.

The original legislation authorized the FSLIC to terminate the insurance of an institution five years after notification "for violation of any provision of this title, or of any rule or regulation made thereunder."[33] This was interpreted in the majority report of the House Committee on Banking and Currency as a basis for issuing regulations for safety. The FSLIC has various powers to deal with the problems of weak associations, including contracting with another insured institution to take over the accounts of an institution in default and creating new federal savings and loan associations with the assets of the old institution.

Legislation in the early 1980s relaxed the distinctions between mutual savings banks and savings and loan associations and between thrifts and commercial banks. Mutual savings banks can now convert to federal charters, and all federally chartered institutions may choose, like commercial banks, a stock form of ownership. Thrifts may diversify outside of housing finance and compete directly with banks for commercial loans and deposits.

Credit Unions

Credit unions are nonprofit institutions that limit their services to members with a "common bond," usually a place of employment but

---

activity was to explain to thrift and home financing institutions the advantages of membership in the Federal Home Loan Bank System and the benefits of Federal Savings and Loan Insurance Corporation coverage. According to the letter this need had largely been met, and furthermore, the funds originally appropriated by Congress for promotion had been depleted. *Federal Home Loan Bank Board and Federal Savings and Loan Insurance Corporation: A Study of Relationships,* Committee Print, Subcommittee on Housing of the Senate Committee on Banking and Currency, 84 Cong. 2 sess. (GPO, 1956), p. 16.

32. 12 U.S.C. 1725.

33. National Housing Act, 48 Stat. 1256, sec. 407(b).

sometimes a much broader link. They arose in the United States as smaller alternatives to savings and loan associations and were chartered by the states. In 1934 Congress authorized the chartering of federal credit unions, extending the dual banking principle already in place for banks and savings institutions.[34] Since 1970, credit unions have been under the jurisdiction of the National Credit Union Administration (NCUA), an independent executive branch agency. Deposit insurance under the National Credit Union Share Insurance Fund (NCUSIF) is mandatory for all federal credit unions and voluntary for those operating under state charter or under the jurisdiction of the Department of Defense. State chartered credit unions also have the option to be insured under the State Share Insurance Fund.

The NCUSIF is in the Treasury Department under the direction of the NCUA board. The board, which charters and supervises federal credit unions, also regulates and examines both federal and state NCUSIF-insured credit unions. Initially the NCUSIF could lend money to troubled credit unions, but this function was taken over in 1978 by the Central Liquidity Facility (CLF). Established under the Financial Institutions Regulatory and Interest Rate Control Act, the CLF is a government corporation managed by the NCUA and capitalized by its member credit unions. Membership in the CLF is open to all insured and noninsured credit unions; credit unions that choose not to become CLF members have access to it through agent members.

Securities Regulation

Federal regulation of securities trading has a shorter history than bank regulation partly because securities markets were not seen to be as critical to the functioning of the economy as banking. Another reason is that commercial and investment banking were indistinguishable for regulatory purposes until passage of the Glass-Steagall Act.

Stock market abuses that were part of the 1930s financial crisis led to the Securities Act of 1933 and the Securities Exchange Act of 1934.[35]

34. Federal Credit Union Act, 48 Stat. 1216. The Farm Credit Administration initially had primary responsibility for federal credit unions. Authority was then placed with the Federal Deposit Insurance Corporation from 1942 to 1947, even though deposits in credit unions were not federally insured. The Federal Security Agency took over in 1947. In 1953, the Bureau of Federal Credit Unions was established in the Department of Health, Education, and Welfare, an arrangement that lasted until 1970, when the National Credit Union Administration was set up.

35. 48 Stat. 74; 48 Stat. 881.

These two laws, which are the foundations of today's regulation, established the Securities and Exchange Commission (SEC) to regulate broker-dealers and the exchanges on which stocks, bonds, and other financial instruments are traded. The Investment Company Act and the Investment Advisor Act, both passed in 1940, extended the SEC's authority to mutual funds.[36]

The regulatory approach of the SEC is different from that of the bank regulatory agencies because the nature of the securities business is different. Customers of securities firms hold claims on underlying assets, not on the firm itself. There is, correspondingly, less concern about the firm's portfolio and more about fraud, conflicts of interest, self-dealing, and other such abuses. Whereas other regulators specify permissible activities for their financial intermediaries, the SEC focuses its efforts more on disclosure, leaving the determination of risk and return to the market. Besides specifying and enforcing public disclosure requirements, the SEC sets rules of conduct for broker-dealers and securities exchanges and assures that the rules of corporate governance permit adequate shareholder participation.

The Securities Investor Protection Corporation (SIPC) is an insurance plan for the protection of customers' funds and securities in accounts at broker-dealers. Created by Congress in 1970 and subject to SEC oversight, the SIPC does not have the federal backing accorded the deposit insurance agencies. Instead, as a mutual, nonprofit, risk-sharing pool it relies on the dispersion of risk among members for its ability to protect investors. The SIPC does not guarantee the value of securities, which would make its coverage analogous to deposit insurance; instead, the coverage protects against loss or theft of the securities or claims against an account.

Although the SEC exercises broad powers, it is largely excluded from one major area—trading in futures and options. The Commodity Futures Trading Commission was set up in 1974 to deal with the rapidly growing volume of business in contracts against future delivery of commodities. Farmers, ranchers, miners, and the manufacturing concerns that rely on agricultural or mineral resources have been actively trading such contracts for more than a century, primarily as a means of hedging risk. More recently, trading has expanded to the extent that investors and speculators with no particular interest in the underlying commodity now predominate. Futures and options have taken on the characteristics of securities.

36. 54 Stat. 847; 54 Stat. 789.

The Commodity Futures Trading Commission is to commodity trading what the SEC is to securities: both agencies must approve proposed new instruments before they can be listed for trading, and both agencies register brokers and oversee the exchanges' regulation of their own members. In addition to its coverage of commodity futures trading, the commission is responsible for stock and bond futures whose price is based on broad market indexes and for options on futures contracts; the SEC is responsible for stock and bond futures based on narrow market indexes and for options on specific securities. Either agency may govern options trading on foreign currencies, depending on whether the transaction occurs on a commodity market or a stock exchange.

The Federal Reserve has a small but important role in securities regulation through its setting of margin requirements—the percentage of a security's value that must be paid for at time of purchase. Through its control of margin requirements, the Federal Reserve is intended to regulate the expansion of credit and to encourage prudent operations. However, only minimum margin levels are set, and much stock trading today is by institutions, which usually do not use credit; thus margin setting is not an effective means of limiting credit, because there is usually substantial unused margin capacity. Moreover, market forces, instead of regulation, are primarily responsible for limiting abuses in margin lending. The Federal Reserve has recently proposed turning over its margin-setting powers to the securities exchanges.

Enforcement of securities registration and disclosure requirements for banks and thrift institutions resides with the institutions' primary regulators, although securities of these institutions' holding companies are covered by the SEC. Securities regulation tends to be reasonably consistent across the agencies, with a few notable exceptions. For example, the rules for banks' common trust funds differ from those applied to the essentially similar mutual funds formed by securities firms.

APPENDIX B

Reform Proposals

THE 1984 recommendations of the Task Group on Regulation of Financial Services, chaired by Vice President George Bush, are only the latest in a long series of reform initiatives. Proposals for overall reform have been made virtually since the moment the first bank regulatory legislation was enacted. Between 1919 and 1921 four separate bills were introduced in Congress to abolish the Office of the Comptroller of the Currency and transfer its supervision powers to the Federal Reserve System. Most of the other proposals put forward by the recent study group have been previously considered as well.

The Brookings Study, 1937

In 1937 the Brookings Institution completed a comprehensive study of the federal bureaucracy under contract for a Senate committee. The report recommended abolishing the Office of the Comptroller of the Currency and giving the Federal Deposit Insurance Corporation, subject to Federal Reserve Board approval, authority to charter national banks.[37] The FDIC was to be accorded veto power over the admission of any state bank to the Federal Reserve System as well as authority to examine all insured banks. The Federal Reserve would have retained the right to make supplementary examinations, when necessary, of member banks and of those applying for Federal Reserve membership. This would have made the FDIC the principal examiner, resolving ambiguities in the original legislation over the examination of member banks and eliminating inefficient duplication of efforts. The reforms were intended to strengthen the FDIC by giving it more power to control the granting of insurance and to investigate the solvency of a bank. Because of its financial stake in the process, the FDIC was thought to place more importance on these activities than the Federal Reserve did.

37. *Investigation of Executive Agencies of the Government,* S. Rept. 1275, 75 Cong. 1 sess. (GPO, 1937), pp. 213–23.

The Office of the Comptroller of the Currency would have been abolished because, of the three agencies, it was regarded as the one with duties most easily transferred. The report stated that further consolidation of regulatory functions into one agency would change the dual nature of the regulatory system, a reform proposal beyond the scope of the study, because it involved political and economic issues rather than considerations of administrative efficiency.

Legislative Proposals, 1938–39

During the next two years, bills were introduced that would have shifted the supervisory functions of the Federal Reserve to the Comptroller of the Currency, creating a new agency called the Federal Bureau of Examination and Supervision. The FDIC would be transferred to a Federal Bureau of Insurance within the Treasury Department.[38] Other bills would have placed all the powers of the Comptroller of the Currency, as well as the regulatory functions of the Federal Reserve, in the FDIC.

The Hoover Commission, 1949

Three reform proposals from separate task forces set up under the Hoover Commission urged the consolidation into the Federal Reserve of the FDIC, the Comptroller of the Currency, or both. The Commission itself rejected all three of these suggestions in favor of a fourth, that of transferring the FDIC to the Treasury Department.

Reorganization Plan No. 2, 1956

Prepared by the Eisenhower administration in accordance with the Reorganization Act of 1956, reorganization plan no. 2 would have separated the Federal Savings and Loan Insurance Corporation from the Federal Home Loan Bank Board (plan no. 1 did not deal with financial regulation).[39] The insurance fund would have been directed by a three-member board of trustees composed of two presidential appointees and the chairman of the FHLBB, ex officio. The FSLIC board would have managed the FSLIC and supervised and regulated insured institutions.

38. GAO, *Federal Regulation of Banks*, p. 8.
39. *FHLBB and FSLIC: A Study of Relationships*, pp. 31–32.

40

The FHLBB was to retain the power to supervise and regulate the federal home loan banks as well as the power to charter, supervise, and regulate federal savings and loan associations. In his message to Congress accompanying the bill, President Eisenhower cited reports by the General Accounting Office and by the Second Commission on Organization of the Executive Branch of the Government. The studies argued that the two agencies should be separated because promoting and chartering federal savings and loan associations conflict with insurance underwriting. The president also noted that the chairman of the FHLBB was to sit on the board of trustees in order to facilitate coordination of FHLBB and FSLIC policies, paralleling the structure of commercial bank regulation. The House and Senate rejected the plan on the grounds that further study should be made before taking action of such major consequence. The House report, which cited the large sums of money involved as reason for caution, also said that recent evidence of lax examinations indicated the need to address the issue.

In the course of the hearings several points had been raised against the case for separation. The concern about conflict of interest was derived from the Bureau of the Budget, which argued that the FHLBB would tend to grant charters to savings and loan associations that could heighten risk exposure for the FSLIC. A staff report by the Senate Subcommittee on Housing argued that a separation of the two organizations along the Comptroller–Federal Reserve–FDIC model would only exacerbate the situation unless the FSLIC were granted power to refuse to insure an association. But the staff report opposed such a separation arrangement—allowing the FSLIC to deny insurance—saying it would cause disagreements over criteria for approval, thereby creating unnecessary conflict and delay; in essence, separation would produce a confusing reversal of the line of power, with the FSLIC able to negate FHLBB actions. According to the staff report, the optimal structure is the one, current then and now, in which the FSLIC has veto power in the granting of charters by the FHLBB if it feels the savings and loan association poses undue risk to the corporation.

Neither the staff report nor the other opponents of separation, the FHLBB and the U.S. Savings and Loan League, addressed supervision, a function that under the reorganization plan would have been accorded to the FSLIC, thereby increasing its control over exposure to risk. The argument against separation presented by the savings and loan league had to do with the inefficiency of creating overlapping functions and additional regulations.

The Commission on Money and Credit, 1961

The next major reform proposal came from the 1961 report of the Commission on Money and Credit, which recommended transferring to the Federal Reserve the supervision function of the FDIC and the Comptroller of the Currency and creating FSLIC insurance for deposits in mutual savings banks.[40] The Commission intended to eliminate the uncoordinated and overlapping activities resulting from the informal arrangements the agencies had developed to fulfill their respective legislative mandates.

H.R. 729 and H.R. 4253, 1963

The first proposal to consolidate the FSLIC and the FDIC was introduced in 1963. The bill, H.R. 729, would have established a Federal Deposit and Savings Insurance Board to manage both insurance funds. The other functions of chartering, regulating, examining, and supervising banks and thrift institutions were not to be affected by the change, except that the new agency would also be in charge of examining and supervising state nonmember savings and loan associations. The FHLBB argued, however, that the proposal would increase inefficiency by splitting federal activities relating to savings and loan associations between two agencies.[41] Also, the fact that the new agency would be forced to develop expertise in the dissimilar banking and thrift sectors would render it less effective.

H.R. 4253, introduced concurrently, proposed consolidating the Comptroller of the Currency, Federal Reserve, and FDIC into a single new agency. The FHLBB favored this bill because it believed that the fragmentation of functions was inefficient, but its stand was moderated by what it regarded as a history of relatively successful coordination among the three agencies.

The Senate Investigation into Federally Insured Banks, 1965

In 1965, the Senate Committee on Government Operations conducted extensive hearings on regulatory consolidation. The leaders of the FHLBB, the FDIC, and the Federal Reserve System attested to the

40. Commission on Money and Credit, *Money and Credit: Their Influence on Jobs, Prices, and Growth* (Prentice-Hall, 1961).

41. *Proposed Federal Banking Commission and Federal Deposit and Savings Insurance Board,* Hearings before the Subcommittee on Bank Supervision and Insurance of the House Committee on Banking and Currency, 88 Cong. 1 sess. (GPO, 1963), pp. 3–165.

problems of split authority in regulation. The FHLBB chairman said the states had been uncooperative in disciplining state chartered associations engaged in illegal or improper practices.[42] The chairman of the FDIC testified that until two years earlier, the Office of the Comptroller of the Currency had consulted with both the Federal Reserve System and the FDIC concerning the approval of charters, even though it was under no legal obligation to do so.[43] He also reported "differences in opinion" that had interfered for approximately a year in the agencies' liaison for bank examination. However, he did not endorse the idea that the three banking regulatory agencies should pool their examination activities. In spite of the difficulties, the FHLBB and FDIC chairmen said that no change was warranted. The Federal Reserve Board chairman, however, was more favorable to the notion of structured change and recommended a comprehensive study on the consolidation of federal supervisory functions.[44] This opinion was echoed by the committee members, who included the consolidation of examination functions in the scope of the study.

The Hunt Commission, 1971

In 1971 one of the most widely recognized studies on regulatory reform was conducted by the President's Commission on Financial Structure and Regulation, more commonly known as the Hunt Commission.[45] The commission recommended that the FDIC, the FSLIC, and the National Credit Union Insurance Fund be incorporated in a Federal Deposit Guarantee Administration, with the funds to remain separate. The Administrator of National Banks, a new organization separate from the Treasury, was to replace the Office of the Comptroller of the Currency and in addition would regulate federally chartered mutual savings banks. The Administrator of State Banks, another new agency, would take from the Federal Reserve the regulation of state chartered, federally insured commercial and mutual savings banks, and from the FDIC its functions except the determination and collection of insurance premiums. Each of the regulatory agencies was granted the right to

42. *Investigation into Federally Insured Banks,* Hearings before the Permanent Subcommittee on Investigations of the Senate Committee on Government Operations, 89 Cong. 1 sess. (GPO, 1965), pt. 1, p. 193.
43. Ibid., p. 159.
44. Ibid., p. 241.
45. *The Report of the President's Commission on Financial Structure and Regulation* (GPO, 1971).

receive the examination reports of other agencies or conduct their own examination of institutions under their jurisdiction.

The criteria used by the Hunt Commission in developing its proposals were as follows: (1) uniformity in the regulation of competing institutions; (2) preservation of the dual system of chartering, examination, and supervision; (3) efficiency; and (4) regulatory specialization in conformity with the specialization of financial institutions.

The Financial Institutions Act of 1973

Many of the Hunt Commission recommendations were later embodied in the Financial Institutions Act of 1973 (S. 2591) and debated in extensive hearings before the Senate Committee on Banking, Housing, and Urban Affairs in 1974. The bill did not contain the Hunt Commission recommendations on structural reform, however, but only those concerning the activities of financial institutions and the chartering of federal mutual thrift institutions.

In one proposal before the Senate Banking Committee, the supervisory authority of the Federal Reserve was to be transferred to the FDIC to allow the former to focus on monetary policy.[46] The proponents noted that there are most commonly two arguments put forth in defense of bank examination by the Federal Reserve: it is necessary for monetary policy formulation, and it is necessary for the proper operation of the discount window. The proponents found neither argument compelling, because the Federal Reserve would under the new system use the reports of the FDIC and states. Futhermore, the Federal Reserve's reports are made at varying points during the year and thus, proponents argued, they cannot properly be aggregated and used in policy formulation. Finally, proponents noted that the Federal Reserve's authority then extended only to state member banks, representing 21 percent of total deposits of insured banks, and was therefore insufficient as a data base.

The Federal Banking Commission, 1973

Even as the Financial Institutions Act was being debated in the Senate, a staff report of the House Committee on Banking and Currency recommended consolidation of the federal financial regulatory agen-

46. "Toward a More Responsive Regulatory Structure," pp. 127–207.

cies.[47] The report proposed a single agency, to be known as the Federal Banking Commission, incorporating the FDIC and the regulatory and supervisory functions of the Comptroller of the Currency and the Federal Reserve. The Treasury would administer the Comptroller's other duties, and the Federal Reserve's activities would be restricted to monetary policy. The plan was intended to cure regulatory laxness, duplication, and waste. Its advocates also hoped that a single federal agency would have smoother relations with state authorities.

Compendium of Major Issues in Bank Regulation, 1975

In 1975 the Chairman of the Senate Banking Committee solicited from nongovernment experts several papers on structural reform. One paper proposed granting the FDIC sole authority to examine banks but did not accord any authority over "charter and branch applications and mergers, except where there is a clear danger to the solvency of a bank."[48] The author vested in the FDIC power to conduct examinations because he regarded it as having the most interest in preventing bank failure. He proposed removing the other functions from FDIC jurisdiction to balance the tendency toward conservatism that would come from its examination responsibilities.

Another study argued that the FDIC should have all regulatory authority over insured banks. Because the greatest percentage of banks falls under the FDIC's responsibilities and because the FDIC bears more of the consequences of bank failure, said the study, the FDIC would have the greatest stake in minimizing banks' risk-taking activities.[49] The paper viewed a centralized system's potential for overly stringent regulation as less costly than the inefficiencies and inconsistencies of the current system.

In arguing for the removal of the examination and supervision functions from the Federal Reserve, the paper said that they divert energy from the Federal Reserve's primary duty—the conduct of mone-

47. *Financial Institutions: Reform and the Public Interest,* Committee Print, Subcommittee on Domestic Finance of the House Committee on Banking and Currency, 93 Cong. 1 sess. (GPO, 1973).

48. George J. Benston, "Bank Examination," in *Compendium of Major Issues in Bank Regulation,* Committee Print, Senate Committee on Banking, Housing, and Urban Affairs (GPO, 1975), p. 585.

49. Charles R. Whittlesey, "Examination and Supervision: Indications and Inferences," in ibid., pp. 611–12.

tary policy—and may also give rise to a conflict of interest. Moreover, the Federal Reserve's role in assuring liquidity is commonly misconstrued as a responsibility for solvency, leading to the mistaken belief that the Federal Reserve must help minimize bank failures through periodic examination and supervision. Instead, the Federal Reserve's mandate requires only access to examination reports that could be prepared by other agencies. Regarding worries about interagency coordination, the study argued that communication between departments of one agency is not inherently more smooth and effective than between two separate organizations.

Another paper renewed the call for a Federal Banking Commission in charge of all regulatory and supervisory activities and organized with a separate division for insurance. Along with the usual arguments of efficiency and consistency was a predominating concern about the current arrangement's tendency toward lax supervision, a problem widely suspected as contributing to the preceding year's failure of two of the largest banks in the United States, Franklin National Bank and the U.S. National Bank of San Diego. Another argument for separating the insurance function from regulation and supervision was that the "least cost" approach for the insurer might not be "least cost" for the economy.[50]

The *FINE* Study, 1975

The next major set of hearings, held in 1975, resulted in four volumes of reports and testimony entitled *Financial Institutions and the Nation's Economy (FINE)*. The *FINE* study was the first to recommend consolidation of all federal bank regulatory agencies into a single new organization. To be called the Federal Depository Institutions Commission, it would assume all functions of the Comptroller of the Currency, the FDIC, FHLBB, and the National Credit Union Administration and the regulatory and supervisory functions of the Federal Reserve. One witness argued that such consolidation should depend on the extent to which banking and thrift institutions become homogeneous in function. As long as savings and loan associations remain the primary source of funds for residential mortgages, there should be an agency such as the FHLBB with the specific responsibility for assuring the even and

50. John E. Sheehan, "1975—The Year for Federal Banking Regulation Reform," in ibid., p. 895.

adequate flow of capital into that market.[51] This theme has been reiterated in the current debate over the proposals of the Vice President's task group. Another witness, who supported the consolidation concept, contended that supervisors were more likely to enforce regulations emanating from their own organization than from one regarded as a competitor. Splitting examination and supervision functions would result in "uninformed supervision and weak examination."[52]

A third witness advocated the functional realignment of the existing agencies in place of the *FINE* study's consolidation proposal.[53] The allocation of duties would be as follows: the Comptroller of the Currency would be responsible for optimizing individual bank performance and would determine permissible activities for banks. The FDIC would be in charge of the safety and soundness of banks; it would have the authority to conduct all bank examinations and to declare banks insolvent. The Federal Reserve System would have jurisdiction over mergers in order to maintain the competitive structure of the banking sector. This regulatory structure differed from the *FINE* proposal's in that the various functions would remain under separate organizations rather than within distinct administrative units of a single agency; it was intended to avoid the concentration of regulatory power and to assure that conflicts in goals between the different functions would be debated openly, with Congress as the final arbiter.

A consumer representative favored consolidation insofar as it could remove resistance to reform in other areas of banking regulation. Because a single agency might be dominated by the commercial banks, however, the consumer advocate proposed the creation of a Federal Banking Agency for Stock Institutions and a Federal Banking Agency for Mutual Institutions. The latter would supervise mutual savings and loans, mutual savings banks, credit unions, and newly created mutual commercial banks.[54]

A contrary view was that federal regulation of savings and loan associations was already too centralized, resulting in repressive supervision. Furthermore, federal authority over the savings and loan industry should not be combined with its authority over the banking sector

51. *Financial Institutions and the Nation's Economy (FINE): "Discussion Principles,"* Hearings before the Subcommittee on Financial Institutions, Supervision, Regulation, and Insurance of the House Committee on Banking, Currency, and Housing, 94 Cong. 1–2 sess. (GPO, 1975), pt. 1, pp. 301–11.
52. Ibid., pp. 318–27.
53. Ibid., pp. 489–93.
54. *FINE*, pt. 2, pp. 926–52.

because that would result in second class status for the savings associations owing to the larger total size of bank assets. Consolidation of the federal insurance functions would still be possible but only if the new insurance agency remained separate from the other federal agencies in charge of chartering, regulating, and examining banks and savings associations. This would avoid any bias toward federally chartered financial institutions by the insurer.[55]

The case against a Federal Depository Institutions Commission was also made by the Comptroller of the Currency, who argued that the division of responsibilities among the three banking regulatory agencies was already efficient enough. He conceded that there was some research and training overlap among the Comptroller, the Federal Reserve, and the FDIC, but he maintained that it could be eliminated if each agency curtailed its own expenditures in these areas. To improve regulatory consistency, he supported a proposal by the Federal Reserve to establish a Federal Bank Examination Council, which would develop uniform standards and procedures for bank surveillance, examination, and follow-up and the review of problem cases. Represented on the council would be the three federal banking regulatory agencies as well as the state regulatory authorities. The Comptroller also recommended that the Federal Reserve designate one member of its board of governors to exercise exclusive authority over bank supervision and to sit as the third member on the FDIC board of trustees.[56]

The Study of Federal Regulation, 1977

In its 1977 *Study on Federal Regulation,* the Senate Committee on Government Affairs proposed a single federal commission for commercial banks that would eliminate the inconsistencies among the Comptroller of the Currency, the Federal Reserve, and the FDIC concerning merger and holding company regulation.[57] The new commission's duties would have encompassed all the examination and supervision functions of the Federal Reserve (except for the regulation of the regional Federal Reserve Banks) as well as the functions of the Federal Reserve board of governors under various banking laws.[58] Under this plan, the Federal

55. Ibid., pp. 844–55, 1224–65.
56. *FINE,* pt. 3, pp. 2411–40.
57. *Study on Federal Regulation,* vol. 5, pp. 197–228.
58. Bank Holding Company Act of 1956, Banking Act of 1933, Securities Act of 1933 and Securities Exchange Act of 1934 (except for margin requirement regulation which would go to the SEC), Consumer Credit Protection Act, Bank Merger Acts, and Edge Act.

Reserve would have retained responsibility for monetary policy, and the chairman of the board of governors was to be permitted to initiate and participate in certain bank commission activities deemed to have an impact on monetary policy. The commission would also have received responsibility for all functions of the Comptroller of the Currency not related to currency issue and redemption (which would be transferred to the Secretary of the Treasury). Similarly, all duties of the board of directors of the FDIC would be transferred. The FDIC would be retained as a corporate entity within the bank commission, automatically granting deposit insurance to all national banks determined to have sound banking practices and to all state banks in states whose banking authorities were considered capable of maintaining safe banking practices. The study proposed a federal reimbursement to encourage state authorities to improve the quality of examination and supervision.

The Consolidated Banking Regulation Act of 1979

A consolidation proposal (S. 332) was introduced to Congress in February 1979 that was less ambitious than the FINE recommendations. Had it passed, it would have placed overall bank regulation in a five-member Federal Bank Commission, but it did not propose changes in the regulation of thrifts or credit unions. Intended to "better insure the safe and sound and competitive operation of the commercial banking system," the Consolidated Banking Regulation Act asserted a need to strengthen the dual banking system and to allow the Federal Reserve to concentrate on its primary responsibility of conducting monetary policy.[59]

The Federal Reserve, the Conference of State Bank Supervisors, and the American Bankers Association opposed the bill, claiming that its concentration of regulatory authority would dampen innovation and that the success of the banking industry showed the adequacy of the current regulatory system. Those opposed to S. 332 argued that, in the previous year, title X of the Financial Institutions Regulation Act established a council to develop coordination among the agencies. The council, consisting of the heads of all of the involved regulatory agencies, had no substantive authority but was designed to be an interim step in the direction of consolidation. Opponents of S. 332 argued that its

59. *Consolidated Banking Regulation Act of 1979,* Joint hearings before the Senate Committee on Governmental Affairs and the Committee on Banking, Housing, and Urban Affairs, 96 Cong. 1 sess. (GPO, 1979).

passage would obviate the council, which they said was an important forum for the exploration of reform alternatives.

The Garn–St Germain Depository Institutions Act of 1982

The Garn–St Germain Depository Institutions Act, passed in 1982, did not change the financial regulatory structure, but it contains provisions facilitating an eventual consolidation of the insurance agencies. The substantial new asset and liability powers it accords thrifts will reduce some of the historical distinctions between banks and thrifts. It liberalized the authority of the FDIC, permitting it to assist weak banks on the same conditions that have applied to FSLIC assistance. Savings banks can convert to federal charters under the Federal Home Loan Bank Board and retain their FDIC insurance. And the bill liberalized chartering of federal associations to reduce the distinctions and barriers between industries.

Recent Reform Proposals

In late 1981 the chairman of the Securities and Exchange Commission called for a comprehensive effort to eliminate anomalies and overlaps in the financial regulatory structure. Repeating his appeal in early 1982 before a Senate committee, the SEC chairman recommended a nonpartisan task force consisting of "experienced executives and recognized authorities" with a one-year mandate to "develop a framework for legislation" to convert from regulation by type of institution to regulation by function.[60] A major result would be to make consistent the regulations that apply to commercial banks, savings and loan associations, and credit unions, all of which receive customer deposits, provide checking services, and make loans. An SEC conference in October 1982 noted that regulation by function would end differences in the treatment of the following pairs of instruments and services: money market funds versus bank deposits, brokerage services offered by banks versus those offered by securities firms, and the registration of offerings of corporate securities by depository institutions versus their holding companies even when the savings and loan or bank may be the holding company's only

60. *Securities Activities of Depository Institutions,* Hearings before the Subcommittee on Securities, Senate Committee on Banking, Housing, and Urban Affairs, 97 Cong. 2 sess. (GPO, 1982), p. 29.

major asset. The notion of regulation by function was embodied in a 1982 bill to establish a commission on capital markets to study the securities activities of commercial banks and to make long-term recommendations.[61]

Task Group on Regulation of Financial Services

The Reagan administration in late 1982 assembled a committee on regulatory reorganization called the Task Group on Regulation of Financial Services.[62] The task group decided to preserve the regulatory structure for savings institutions, but eligibility for regulation as a bank or thrift would be determined by looking at an institution's asset portfolio; if there was an insufficient proportion of mortgage loans, the institution would be defined and regulated as a bank regardless of its charter.

The task group proposed more substantial changes for bank regulation. The Office of the Comptroller of the Currency, to be renamed the Federal Banking Agency, would retain its current powers over national banks plus authority over most bank holding companies. The Federal Reserve would retain its regulation of only those bank holding companies comprising about fifty of the largest banks, which account for about one-third of the assets of the country's 14,000 banks. To the Federal Reserve the FDIC would give its supervisory and examination powers over all but problem banks. Enforcement of other laws that are now the responsibility of the bank and thrift regulatory agencies would be transferred to the Department of Justice (antitrust), the Securities and Exchange Commission (securities), and the Federal Trade Commission (consumer protection).

A measure of the task group's difficulties in reaching a consensus can be seen in the apparent inconsistency between proposed bank and thrift regulatory structures—a unified regulatory structure for the thrift industry and multiple agencies for banks. Thus the potential for regulatory conflicts, while reduced, would nevertheless remain. The Federal Re-

---

61. H. Res. 7014, *Congressional Record,* daily edition (August 18, 1982), p. H6524.

62. *Blueprint for Reform: The Report of the Task Group on Regulation of Financial Services* (GPO, 1984). Led by Vice President George Bush, the group consisted of the secretary of the treasury, the attorney general, the assistant to the president for policy development, and the heads of the Commodity Futures Trading Commission, the Council of Economic Advisers, the FDIC, the FHLBB, the Federal Reserve Board, the NCUA, the SEC, the Office of the Comptroller of the Currency, and the Office of Management and Budget.

serve, the new Federal Banking Agency, and state agencies would all have authority over bank holding companies, necessitating coordination that is not required under the current system, wherein control is centralized in the Federal Reserve. Even the Federal Banking Agency's authority to define permissible activities for holding companies would be constrained by the possibility of a Federal Reserve veto. Moreover, despite the transfer of routine regulatory powers away from the FDIC, that agency would still be able to use insurance regulations as a means of controlling the activities of insured banks. Thus the task group proposal leaves unresolved many points of contention among agencies.

A simpler plan would have had the Federal Reserve's regulatory powers transferred entirely to the new Federal Banking Agency, but the Federal Reserve argued strongly for retaining some jurisdiction.[63] The Federal Reserve has long maintained that the regulation of depository institutions (primarily banks) affects monetary stabilization, and therefore the central bank should have some regulatory authority.

63. See Board of Governors of the Federal Reserve System, "Federal Reserve Position on Restructuring of Financial Regulation Responsibilities" (December 1983).